Maddy's
I Am Here

The Memoirs of Madalyn

The Memoirs of Madalyn

MADALYN MYERS

CITIOFBOOKS, INC.
3736 Eubank NE Suite A1
Albuquerque, NM 87111-3579
www.citiofbooks.com
Hotline: 1 (877) 389-2759
Fax: 1 (505) 930-7244

Ordering Information:
Quantity Sales. Special discounts are available on quantity purchases by corporations, associations, and others. For details, contact the publisher at the address above.

Printed in the United States of America.

ISBN-13   Paperback   978-1-963209-20-4

Library of Congress Control Number: 2024900120

Contents

Maddy I am real

Maddy I'm just Madalyn

Define Maddy: Classy, Elegant, and True

Maddy say's, My laws my way!

Maddy is at her best but not easily broken

Our lives are as beautiful as

God's footprints in the sky

When we learn to love ourselves!

I believe that God does not crucify

His followers only strengthens them

So I shall continue my written success!

Incerpt

This is my life story in a bundle. All the joy, luck, love and not so good times. There were times that I wanted to live and there were times I wanted to die. So this book is dedicated to those people who said good bye to death, looked in the mirror and said I Am here!

Acknowledgements

I would like to acknowledge the God of our universe and all his love, wisdom, and understanding. Thank you Jesus for everything including the confidence to write this book.

My three children Frederick Myers, Harmony Myers, and Gwen Ankomah.

My Dad Amon Emanuel Myers, love ya! Also my mom Gwendolyn Newman who still inspires me from the other side who is now deceased. Mom always said you are going to make it while Dad always say you are a lady. My brothers Althonso, Darrell, and Donald for always keeping a close eye on me. My sister Angel for her love and good intellect.

Also to my entire family for visiting me when I was in the hospital and praying and leaving a door open for the spirit of God to come rescue me and save me in mind body and spirit. My nephfew Chris and to my best and dear friend Marco who gave me hope and inspiration when needed.

Most of all my divine appointed angels who love me and help me everyday.

Complete thought

Mocason Son

Safe Haven My eye is on the sparrow

I can take it my heart is at ease

Like a swan I follow you through the shadows and water

My heart is you

My love is you, Mocason Son

Speak to my heart holy one and

Like a dove you are pure

My light grows as I follow you through heaven

You cover me and lead me to divine wholeness

The most High and beloved King Jesus!

Thank you
Love Madalyn

Chapter 1

Ashamed

I am here today and pray fully many tomorrows. In this biography I am just taking a few meditating deep breaths so that I can imagine this moment is real. I am actually writing a book. I have feared writing and showing it to others when my ninth grade English instructor advised me that poets don't make a lot of money. So by God's grace I have defeated the enemy and faced my fear of writing and typing. I dropped out of high school at age sixteen. I received my GED at age nineteen and that took confidence. I will get back to that story later on in the chapters. I was eight years old when I saw my self as a victim for the first time in my life. I walked into our court yard of our apartment complex in South East Washington D.C. and I witnessed a crack head woman being beaten and dragged down the steps in front of an apartment building. Three drug dealers were beating her black and blue for not paying them money she owed them. I remember walking past fast paced and afraid. Things like this happened in the heart of the ghetto back in 1988. My mother three older brothers and oldest sister lived in a two bedroom apartment back then. I was the youngest out of the five of us. Being a latch key kid I walked home and I kept the house key on a shoe string to let myself in to our home everyday after school. Seeing the woman being beaten I remember saying this would not ever be me. I also had a lot of bullies in school, and not many friends. My father was a disabled veteran and alcoholic, him and mom split when I was 5 years old. My father was not a man who physically abused us but he would call the house and aggravate my mother by saying he wanted me to live with him when he was drunken. Dad would come over and listen to music, nag Mom, and hold me on his lap. He always said each visit that if some

1

one ask who you are what do you say? Then I always was taught by Dad to call myself a lady. Amon Myers is my fathers, name he is six foot three inches and always kept clean manicured nails. He always dressed nice and kept a half pint of whiskey in his back pocket. My mother Gwendolyn Newman was five nine and a half and she was a pretty brown skin woman. She was a happy loving and caring heavy set woman. O God was she honest she hated if anyone lied to her. We moved out of the ghetto by the time I turned nine years old and into a middle class suburb in Landover M.D. I was very happy and excited because we had a three bedroom apartment with two bathrooms. I had a lot of neighborhood friends and a playground right across the street where my mother could walk out of the building and see me playing. I grew up a little too fast in Landover by learning how to curse with friends chase boys and sneak out when on punishment. I was on the neighborhood cheerleading squad, school talent shows, and class field trips. My mom started working as a custodian for the government building in downtown D.C. so we had more advantages than before when we lived in the projects. I still got into fights at school but we would be friends again sooner or later. I remember becoming friends with two twins down the street from my house. They were from Alabama and one of them became my best friend. She was the bomb I was light skin and she was dark skin we were like night and day. Actually she was the one who told me when I started my period at age eleven. She had already started her period at age nine. Even though I had a best friend I did not know what love felt like. I thought love meant saying thank you or giving my mother a kiss on the cheek, or just being around my Aunts and cousins. I later in life learned what true love meant and who I should depend on most in the sixth grade I was about 98 pounds and five foot six inches tall. I was ashamed of my height and I was probably the tallest girl in my class, on the squad, or just in general. This is what I felt like at least most of the time. My breast were an A cup and I had to finally wear bras. The boys at school called me too tall. I was always called big nose by the bullies but I just would fight and move on. At my sixth grade graduation I was happy, my father took me to get a new haircut and style that would set a trend for my teen years. My haircut was in a page boy like Halle Berry one of my role models and I also wore my first pair of high heels outside of trying on my Mothers heels. My dress was red and I wore a choker around my neck as fashion.

My best friend one of the twins showed up at my front door the morning our graduation dressed in all white and the first thing she said is you are so pretty. For the first time in my life I felt beautiful. She was like a angel because she would fight for me and she always said nice things to me and very seldom stayed angry with me for long. I know one thing I rocked that hair cut from sun up to sun down. I started wearing daisy dukes by age twelve and attracted older males. This new image gave me power and I liked it I felt like a grown up most days. But now at home my brother Althonso got into more trouble and hung out in the street playing hooky at school and chasing females. One day he got caught in a shoot out and got shot at six times and all of the bullets missed him. He had a pair of baggy used jeans on that day and the jeans caught the bullets and missed his skinny legs. Althonso next to me the youngest had been arrested, sold drugs, and always kept a girlfriend. He dropped out of high school and got his barbers license and help Mom pay bills. Darrell was like our father figure at times and cooked for us and watched us when Mom was at work, the third child down from the oldest. Darrell went with the flow dated with good jobs and was basically the man of the house. Darrell was a ladies man and kept a good job. H e stopped his schooling in the eleventh grade and kept working. Donald my eldest brother stayed in the streets liked big boned women and was always breaking rules. Donald dated women who were plain meaning no hair do, odd, and big. Donald would be in and out of the house mostly. I do know that he kept up on us about school. Donald left school in the eleventh grade too. My sister Diane we called her Angel was scary as hell. She was always screaming at us fighting everyone including Mom, and she was the first one to get married and move out of the house which left me with three big feet brothers and Angels son my little nephew Chris. Mom raised Chris so he was like an annoying little brother. Mom worked a lot and I wanted a lot of things she could not afford sometimes. I learned how to cook from watching Darrell and Mom. I knew how to bake cookies, cakes, and hotdogs, macaroni and cheese and noodles by age twelve. I used to love My mothers cooking and watching her cook made me happy. She would ask me to help her on holidays. Chris would run around play Nintendo and ask me thousands of questions that I did not care to answer. So we were one big happy family. I thank God for them because they help nurture and shape me into a woman with good values. I feel like I grew

3

up fast and learned a lot early on, but it does not change where I grew up and came from. In school I loved to read and write. My Mother always brought me books home to read and kept up on me about my grades. My Mother had grew up in a house with nine other siblings with her made ten children. A lot of my aunts and uncles had to work versus go and finish high school. So Mom help me keep focused each day and I really appreciate her warm heart and love.

Chapter 2

Afraid

Leaving Landover M.D. was not easy I was twelve years old when we moved and majority of my friends were there. My sister had gotten married and moved in with her husband and children, Chris moved along with us. Babysitting became a weekend job for me and I learned how to take care of small children by watching my nieces and nephew for Angel. Becoming independent felt good and I loved to have money to go shopping. Fonzo lost his best friend in a shooting incident so he continued to work and help Mom out. Darrell had moved in with his girlfriend at the time and Donald had moved out on his own as well. So that left Chris, Mom, Fonzo, and I in an apartment in Forestville M.D I remember that was the first time in my life that I experienced depression. I remember going to school and stressing out a lot about my appearance. Getting teased was not fun I went home and cried my eyes out plus prayed to God that I could get a new hip wardrobe. With fate being so good my Father would bring me money seasonal to help pay for clothes. I then began getting my hair cut, colored, and styled by Fonzo girlfriend as practice while she attended cosmetology at her high school, so I was set. I know with all of these positive changes in my life came trouble. I attracted older guys sometimes men. Dad visits were less frequent and I remember feeling lonely and sad sometimes. I dated a guy that was eighteen and lost my virginity to him after two months of dating. Boy was I young and dumb. I was not in love but some of the girls at school talked of having sex and I wanted something to brag about as well. I now wish I had waited. I remember my stomach feeling like it was filled with air as he tried to penetrate and I did not bleed much. In my mind I felt like a grown up and it felt like he cared about me but he didn't. A few

5

weeks later he was telling his friends about our ordeal and started dating an older girl across the street from us. I eventually moved on and dated a guys but had no sex for a while. Toni Braxton was real hot back then and I tried to imitate her style to attract the older guys. I started shaving my legs, keeping my hair wrapped and curled, and wearing mini skirts. I bought Toni Braxton tapes and sang along with her music word for word. By then girls at school said I thought I was cute and the boys stop calling me big nose so I was happy. Halle Berry was also an idol during this time they were sexy and independent so I wanted to be beautiful and rich like them. My zodiac sign is cancer so I loved good cooking especially macaroni & cheese, looking good, and smelling good. I know this was the fisrt time in my life that I began to learn that prayer works. Inspite of me being permiscuous I still learned how to ask God for his help. My Mother was prayer filled and she loved singing in church. Every one said she sounded like Aretha Franklin which she did. Any time she got angry and wanted the house clean we always heard this speech "I did not raise a bunch of fu***** drop outs I could have left all of yall as*** outside on the curb like this woman did her kids and get me a singing career". After this speech the house was spotless. Until this very day I can't stand a dirty house. Whoop there it is! So when I turned thirteen I knew how to stay home take care of the house while Mom worked and watch Chris. I know I was a little conceited too, because I had more of a woman's attitude toward life and not the head of a teenager. Fonzo and I had fights about me dating older guys but he never told Mom. Telling Fonzo's baby mama all my secrets while getting my hair done was crazy. She always told Fonzo even though I was a babysitter and all that. My boobs were now a size b cup so I had something to push up every so often and I did try to accent those as well. Having had my first yeast infection was not fun at all. The doctor looked in between my legs and said something like yeah it looks pretty yeasty then prescribed my Mom some gyenelotrium. I was very scared and embarrassed, when I told my best cousin the news she was like ill gross with your yeasty ass. My cousin was the same height one year older than me wore the same haircut but she stayed a virgin. We joined the choir and had choir rehearsal on Saturdays. That was fun and We went to different churches in D.C. to perform and sing with Donald Vails youth choir Capital City. My cousin and I caught the subway cracked jokes, laughed at every thing possible.

By then we both met our boyfriends in another choir and we really got in a hot seat. I stayed kissing and rubbing with him and I also felt like I cared about him more than anything at that time in my life. Mom and my aunt joined the adult ministries and choir, they knew that my Cousin and I had these boyfriends but they did not suspect that we would sneak off during church to get a quick kiss or rub in.

Turning fourteen was hard. I had slept with Jay my boyfriend at the time and he actually felt like my first because we dated for a few months and had feelings for each other. He called me everyday after school or I called him. Fonzo had went to jail for assault against some guy who he had beef with. I was afraid and sad deep inside but being so young I never knew that by my brother going to prison this had really brought on an abandonment issue with male figures in my life. So myself, Chris, and Mom stayed together by now. Jay was like the only outlet emotionally that I could cling to. We talked about getting married and I longed to be loved. I remember that having my own family and security would make me happy. Writing poems, love letters, or singing became a positive outlet and school was alright but I still had this issue with myself. Inspite having of friends and Jay becoming possessive I still felt like I had to take care of others never really myself. This is who I was a nurturer but I never really had childhood. I wanted to be with Jay all the time. By him being seventeen he was around older girls all the time and I was so broken hearted when he took a girl to the prom and not me. That crushed me I again experienced depression and went into my shell. I no longer had his over protective jealous attitude which really kept me on my toes, anymore. He started to lose interest after dating a older woman. Crying a lot after losing him became painful. Getting a cocker spaniel two weeks old made me feel like a mother and after about three months of being depressed sleeping with men just came easy after that. I was trying to replace Jay by sleeping with guys that made me feel good. I became very insecure with myself plus being that way was away to mask being afraid of being hurt or left alone.

7

The Game

The Game it's a shame how our love went up in flames

The Game it's a shame how our love is not the same

The Game it's a shame our love was blind so goodbye

I don't want you cause what you put me through

I am no longer happy with you

We were two of a kind

But you were no longer mine

Baby don't call my name

I am not to blame

You are not my friend

So this is the end

Don't call me or page me

This thing called love is crazy

You got to much game

So stay the same without me

Goodbye!

Chapter 3
Aggressive

I remember that I went to my brothers home for the holidays about four months of breaking up with Jay. I was taking a bath and I remember scratching a lot in the tub. I picked at my pubic hair and pulled out a crab. I began to scream and my brothers wife came into the bathroom to see what was going on. She yelled oh my God you have lice. I began crying and she said have you had sex. I was so scared and I told her not recently. She said well you can get them from the public restroom. She also told me that the lice can jump at least nine feet from the toilet. Honey I had to shave my private parts, and they had to buy me a lice kit. I was so ashamed but I did go to a local mall and use the restroom a week prior to the visit at my brothers house. Everything in the house had to be disinfected and sprayed. I went to school after the holidays and was no longer depressed. My dog Lucky was getting bigger and followed me around everywhere. I dated a twenty four year old man who sold drugs and he wanted to get married but I was afraid to get married by that time. He bought me shoes and clothes and payed for hotel rooms from time to time. I grew to be five feet nine inches tall so no one questioned my age when we went out. The relationship lasted about three months and I did not regret being with him at the time. My style in clothes changed and I became obsessed with wearing high heels everywhere. Whether the heels were boots or sandals I did not care. My hair color was jet black and I loved mini skirts. My career goal was to be a model because I received so many compliments on my height and weight of 136 pounds. Watching music videos of various artist from Brandy, Tamia, Monica, Usher and anyone elsc back in 1995 became one of my best hobbies. I also began to study astrology and read about zodiac signs. I even purchased a quiga board and asked it questions about love or anything. Once over a friends house the board spelled out the word beheaded and my two friends and I began crying. So I gave the game away. Mom and I grew closer together but we had a lot of disagreements when turning fifteen approached. We had disagreements about my dress code but I shaved and wore mini skirts anyway. Chris and I fought about him coming in my room when I had my cousin or friends over the house, He was just annoying always back then. We had moved to Greenbelt M.D. and Mom got a section 8 voucher so we was able to afford a nicer apartment. I was very happy and so was my Mother. My Mother purchased a new car so we were in a good suburb and life was great. My high school was right across the street and I could walk to school. No longer living in D.C. I left Capital City youth choir and joined the choir at my school. My hair started to grow and I got my hair in braids like Brandy. Eye liner and lip gloss was my make up selection and I also learned how to add my own weave to my hair. I know that being fifteen brought on a lot of emotions. PMS was a very big deal, and I began having a lot of mood swings. I woke up every morning and never ate breakfast or lunch at school. So I would come home and eat as soon as I entered the house. My dog sat and looked at me the whole time so he would eat with me. Mom only required that Chris and I keep the house cleaned up and don't have company while she wasn't at home. I eventually got a part time job at pizza hut and I worked for four hours after school. Being independent felt great and I could shop at the beauty store or go to Ross to buy name brand clothes for cheap. I was popular at my new school and was nominated for best dressed. I became very vain and my appearance mattered more to me than getting to school on time. I met a guy at pizza hut and he got me into drinking alcohol and staying out late, he was cute but I was not attracted to him physically.

I started having issues being at home and having responsibilities to my home life. I became a people person and I loved to go hang out a lot. I dropped out of the pom pon squad at school and I would go jogging at the school track on weekends. I watched my weight a lot and I loved to look thin. I remember that I would come home and eat a cup of melted cheese that I would bring home from pizza hut and eat it by itself. It would taste so good and I would be happy with just that cheese for dinner. Mom took me to several modeling schools and we did not have the money to go far with them and that hurt. So investing in black hair magazines or just any magazine kept me up with the latest trend. After along school year of fashion, fun, dances, and talent shows. I was ready to turn sixteen, Babysitting was out of the question I did not want to have any children by that time or keep any ones children, I was just totally against it. I did still go out on dates and that was fun. I changed jobs and began to smoke weed by the summer of 1996. Cigaretts was another hobby of mine. I cut my hair again after growing it out and worked a lot. I also found masturbation to be an outlet. My mind stayed on money mostly and my friendships got less and less and dating seemed more fun. The guy that was my friend at pizza hut loved to get drunk and get me drunk. I was the one he took to his prom but still no sex between us. He did not smoke weed just drink and kid around half the time. But still during the fall of that year school seemed less and less important to me. My boyfriend whom I met at our local fashion show became very possessive and verbally abusive. He hated the fact that I smoked weed, drank, and hooked school. So he cursed me out a lot actually all the time and I put up with him anyway. He was my first when it came to having oral sex so I believe that he kept his grips on me with that. Money was not an issue because I kept a job even though I did not like school. School just was boring as hell to me and hanging out with the older crowd seemed more exciting. We moved from Greenbelt to Laurel where half of my friends from our old neighborhood seemed to follow us. By that time I had to repeat the eleventh grade because I got thrown out of summer school. I found another job at Mc Donalds and began to work more and roam the new neighborhood looking for the weed and hotspots. I really enjoyed being high and it made me feel better. Going swimming and getting high was like a ritual during the summer at that point. I would spend a night with my boyfriend over his cousin house quite often and that made me happy. I was not very depressed at the time. I soon bought a fake I.D. and started working at a strip club near by in Laurel. It was on I went to school and was a stripper on weekends. I then smoked more and drank more to motivate myself to strip. When my boyfriend found out he just treated me with more disrespect. I did not care and I eventually quit going to school and stripped full time. Mom had no idea at all that I stop working and going to school to strip. I was crazy and I started to keep secrets from my mother. I also used to shop lift every so often. The odd thing is that no one in my neighborhood knew at the time that I took my clothes off for a living. So I kept on living like it was a normal profession. Not for a sixteen year old well by then I had already turned seventeen. Still I was living the life of an adult. I had people that were so called friends and this made matters worse. I began to see less and less of Mom and she got tired of yelling at me everyday. I would leave two hundred dollars on the dresser every now and then while she slept and go on with my night. Chris smoked weed by then and became a problem as well as myself but Mom just dealt with us. I thank God for her until this day and I hope that I can be as strong as she was back then. My Mother took to my life style I know through prayer and even though Fonzo went to prison she still supported him through prayer and faith. Dad would call and check on me sparingly, He also would stop bye our home when needed. My brothers and sisters shared the same Mother but we did not share the same father. But Fonzo still had our support. I soon met a new man that was twenty seven and also sold drugs. We had got introduced through mutual friends. He had money all the weed I wanted to smoke and a car which was alright to me because I did not drive or carry a drivers license at the time. He was real thick built and took me every where I wanted or needed to go. We went out to eat a lot and stayed at motels every night. I remember feeling that this is cool. Sex was great and I got over my last break up rather quickly by spending so much time with someone new. He stayed at the strip club sold drugs and would take me out after my time to leave the club every night. I gained ten pounds and my breast became even larger. A lot of the women in the club began to talk badly about me cause being with him brought me more money and a lot more attention. I really did not care because I was happy everything was going my way. By this time I would go home maybe twice a week and stay with him the remaining week. I smoked weed from sun up until sun down and my alcohol consumption was straight liquor no chaser. I would fill my cup with vodka or cognac and that would get me through each day at the club. Getting alcohol was not a problem because all my friends were twenty one or older. One of the girls at the club got me started snorting kay and dropping ecstacy pills from time to time. Her and I grew real close so then I began traveling with her to Baltimore to strip out there as well. My wardrobe was nice I kept the nicest wigs and I stayed with the latest trends by keeping money. I tried going to a class to take my GED but I dropped the class after two months and kept stripping. I ate out all the time and got my nails and toes done every two weeks. I was having a good time and things seemed to be flowing right. I turned eighteen and went salsa dancing to celebrate with a woman who lived in my neighborhood. She sold her body but did not work at the club. Her and her boyfriend got into a huge fight that night and my birthday was ruined. The saddest part was that her boyfriend wanted to turn on me and fight but I walked off. From that day forward this woman became bad news. She turned tricks, borrowed my clothes, and kept confusion going. She even tried to sleep with my man but he wasn't having it. I know that I hung around her and became very insecure with my self. Only God knows how jealous she became of me and my life. My other friends would say leave her alone she is a leach. She had no job and an apartment she could not afford. She slept with men to pay her bills. I remember one night I went out with her and her cousin and we met a guy driving and followed him to a party. I was the only one drinking that night. We had gotten some weed and I help roll blunts to smoke. In the bottom of the bag I noticed this crystal like substance and when I asked what it was one of the guys at the party snatched it out of my hand. We smoked so much that night I did not even realize that the laced weed was for me. She had set me up I went back home that night and woke up the next morning afraid of everything. I kept praying and would not leave my room. My mother went out of town to a gospel convention in New Orleans and was not due back for a week. I was paranoid forgetting where I put something last and I was very angry for no reason. My old friend from pizza hut stop by to see me and was scared to death at how I acted in front of his friends. I finally broke down and called my father to come and pick me up from home. I began to hear voices and would jump at any loud noises. Dad came to get me and Chris then fifteen went over our neighbors house. Dad drove to his house and he knew something was wrong. I walked around in circles and I began to become mute. My Grandma said this child acts like she scared or something. My father said I'm taking you to get a drug test. I did not even notice him at times. The next day I overheard my Father say who did this to my baby. I began to cry and he said get in the car. I'm taking you to the shop. We rode over to one of Dad's best buddies car shop and I began to panic. Thoughts raced through my mind and would not stop. The radio I thought was the voice of God speaking to me. As soon as my Fathers friend approached

15

the car I began to scream and cry and I got out of the car and ran. Luckily Dad had already called the paramedics before we left the house. The cops and paramedics caught a hold of me before I ran into the middle of the street facing oncoming traffic. They grabbed me then gave me a strong sedative to calm me down before putting me into the ambulance. In my mind the ambulance was taking me to hell where I would get burned, beat, and then raped. I was so scared I started to cry. When inside the hospital a male nurse asked me do you know where you are, Yes I replied in heaven. That was the last thing I remember until the next day in the hospital. When I woke up my wig was gone I lost that the previous night wrestling the paramedics. A catheder was in my urine tract, when I felt it it hurt and yanked it out. A doctor came in the room and said I should have ask someone to remove the catheder, Then she said do you know why you are here. I said no, then she went on saying that you have pretty large amounts of PCP in your system. That did not seem right to me because I never willingly took PCP so that meant someone whom I smoked weed with laced my blunt. I had no idea what so ever of who would do this to me. Three of my Aunts walked in shortly afterwards to pick me up from the hospital in Cheverly M.D. and we rode back to my house. Mom was still in New Orleans for the gospel convention. I was afraid of loud noises and I wanted a cigarette badly. I did not want to go with my Aunts to there house then I couldn't smoke weed or drink. So I called my brothers wife to pick me up. We went to their house and I really became an emotional wreck. I walked around in circles and look at myself in the mirror. My attention span was very low and all I did was smoke cigarettes. I looked bad my hair was all over the place and I became afraid to talk to people. The more people I saw the more I became afraid and would say to my brother and his wife I am scared. They would often ask who did this to you tell us, but I was just mute. My Father called sparingly to check on me. I would ask to smoke weed but my brother told me no. My nephew Chris eventually got picked up from the house and he did not understand why I became mute. My eyes began to get sunken in and dark circles appeared around my eyes. I lost weight because I could not eat nor sleep. I began to hate everyone because of the way I looked and felt. When my brother found out my boyfriend who sold drugs. He initially thought he set me up, so my brother called him over to the house. He also called my cousin to meet him at the house. When my brother pulled up at the house him and my cousin jumped out of the car. My boyfriend was about to get jumped and beat up pretty badly until I said he did not give me the PCP. That is when the girl who I thought was such a good friend and I went to the party with her that night became my worst enemy. My boyfriend was so scared that before he left he said I told you to stop hanging out with that trifling bitch. I could not move my mouth to say anything. Each day I got worse and was very nervous. In one week I lost twenty pounds, my mouth was red from drinking red juice. I looked like a damn zombie. This had to be the worst time of my life. I then smoked a joint with my brothers wife which he knew nothing about and I went crazy. I thought God was every where and I became afraid that he would send me to hell. God is every where but I was going through hell. My Mom came back from vacation and I was not the daughter that she had before she left. My mind was gone and I had about as much sense as a four year old. Every one had to tell me when eat, sleep, or bathe. All day I walked around the house and looked in the mirror afraid of my own reflection. One day my Mom dropped me off at my brother house and He told me to stop smoking so many cigarettes, I went on his patio to smoke and I thought the world was coming to an end. I ran back in the house and my brother then went outside on the patio. I ran into the kitchen thinking that demons were chasing me so I grabbed a steak knife slit my wrist and began stabbing myself in the chest. I stabbed myself twelve times and began screaming. My brother heard his wife and I screaming and the children crying and ran in to see what happened. He grabbed the knife out of my hand and pick me up and put me in the bath tub. I remember my brother crying saying Precious please breath. That was a nick name my Mom gave to me when I was born. Again the ambulance was called and I was flown to the hospital.

.

Chapter 4

Momma you are divine

Momma it's your time

To be seen upon the world

You know I'm your Baby girl

Momma I love you so much

By you I'll always be touched

I thank God for you

Rest well in heaven and stay true

Momma I'll always love you

By: Precious AkA Madalyn

My Doctor told Mom that I had repeatedly stabbed my self and would need immediate surgery in order for me to live. She was notified at her job of what had happened to me. My lungs, kidneys, and liver were punctured due to the stabbing. When I awoke in the hospital days later, My upper torso was wrapped in bandages. Tubes were also taped to the sides of my body, and a machine constantly pumped fluid in and out of my body. I remember screaming and yelling trying to snatch the tubes out from my side, So several nurses ran in the room to grab my hands and sedate me. When a sleep I awoke to see my Mom, brother, cousins, aunts, and uncles all staring into the glass window at me. I said nothing, all I could do was lie on my back with broken ribs due to surgery. Another day I awoke and saw one of my Aunts reading the bible over top of me while my Mother sat at her side. It seemed as if the days went by fast and each day through prayer things began to come together. Being in shock I still could not speak for at least two and a half weeks. I still was not myself. Dad came to visit me and could not stay long seeing me in such critical condition. My room was filled with balloons, baskets, and fruit each day brought in by my family. I was amazed but still sick mentally. Mom looked hurt and began to lose weight a little. I was very afraid, scared, and angry. I thought bad thoughts daily. I could not shower, or shampoo my hair with out the help of hospital staff. I felt sad, lonely, and very depressed. From the time this tragedy happened I was never the same. One day I snatched the tube out of my side but the machine was off and I was healed so I did not bleed. I was then sent to the psychiatric ward in the hospital and treatment began there. My Mom came everyday and showed me home videos of myself dancing and laughing with Chris. She also showed up at the hospital one day and told me you are going to tell the world one day what happened to you. I weighed one hundred and twenty seven pounds at the time. I went to groups and meetings at the hospital until I was released. When I got home family still came by and I was afraid to go for walks by myself. So I went everywhere with Mom. Love came easy and I actually listened to her every word. She said that if she did not work so much then none of this would have happened. All I could say was I should have listened to you when you warned me to stay out of the street. Mom and I went every where and stayed together after that. My old boyfriend never came to see me once while I was in the hospital. Neither did any of my so called friends at the club come by, No one but my family the people I ran away from mostly. I went back to school to finish the eleventh grade and I weighed about one hundred and sixty four pounds. I took at least five different medications at the time. All prescribed for either depression or mood stabilizers. I felt very fat and ugly. This was the biggest I had weighed all my life. I went into a shell and stayed depressed everyday. Three months later I smoked weed again and began to hang out with guys in the neighborhood. When Mom found out she said are you trying to kill me or something. I Then saw the hurt in her eyes and felt the pain in her heart and began to cry. She helped me get into rehab the spring of year 2000 and I went. I stayed there about fourty five days and left with a man I started dating three months prior to me entering rehab. I moved in with him in spite of my mother's warning not too. I lived with him eight months and got pregnant with my first child. Living with him was painful, We fought all the time and He always verbally abused me. I became very insecure and moved back home with Mom. We lived in District Heights M.D. at this time and I was happy to be home. Mom had surgery on her breast but said it was just a knot. I got even fatter due to the pregnancy and I feared being a Mom. Mom kept me happy by just being there we never argued anymore and I appreciated her even more. Mom went in the hospital and had another surgery on her left lung. Half of her lung had to be cut off due to cancer which I knew nothing about. She never told me anything about having cancer. She came home and help me get through being pregnant and I helped her recover from surgery. Mom got well slowly and I became even larger from eating everything she cooked. The food was good and I did not care how I looked. My hair stayed done and I gained about fourty five pounds in addition to my one hundred and sixty pound frame. I decided to name my daughter Harmony Sabrina Myers. She was seven pounds ten ounces. I had not smoke any weed or drank any alcohol for about a year and a half now. Harmony was a jewel she made me so happy. She had colic really bad and cried a lot but I still remained clean. My brother Darrell would watch Harmony and help me and my Mom as well. Mom was happy to have us around her again. As Harmony grew Mom seemed to cough a lot more and she didn't seem to have as much energy. I suffered from depression and my psychiatrist prescribed a anti depressant for me to take. It helped a lot but still Mom was not herself at times. I went to church with her when she sang her solo

21

in the choir Genesis two. She was even crying while talking to my Aunt one day in the living room of our home. Lord knows I had no idea that the cancer was as severe as it was at the time. We went to the clinic to find out that she needed radiation treatment to try and stop the disease from spreading. She went for about six weeks, and I would normally tag along. I started receiving a check each month from the welfare office to help me with Harmony, so I stayed home to take care of her. Mom also gave me money to go to drivers education so that I could get my drivers license. I passed the test the first time and I was so excited. One of my Aunts passed away and her funeral was held at Jericho Baptist church on nine eleven. The same day the World Trade Center was blown up. I became restless at home so I started to attend church and Bible study each week. I saw less and less of Harmony's father by then. We were ready to move so I started looking in the apartment guides for a new apartment. Mom went to the hospital in April of 2002 and stayed in the hospital. I had to drive to appointments by then and I found a realtor that helped with the search for an apartment. Darrell was upset and so was I about Mom being ill. I thought that like the previous times she would get well but she only got worse. Chris went to job corp and I stayed pretty close to my Aunt and cousins. We found a place to live in Reston Virginia and it was so nice to live at a distance from the areas where I grew up. Fonzo would call from jail upset that our Mother was sick, and dying from cancer. Harmony was eleven months when my Mother passed away June 1, 2002. I was on my own and I was scared. I had to get food stamps and medical assistance for us because I was not working at the time. I loved Virginia though it was very peaceful and that is where I began to find out who I really was internally. My Aunt advised me to attend cosmetology school and I did. I enrolled Harmony in day care and went to school in Falls Church. I stayed in school and that help me with depression of losing my Mother. I know that I cried a lot and I talked on the phone to family to keep myself focused. I also would drive out to D.C. in order to visit my family on weekends. Harmony was like an Angel that God had sent to keep me busy and happy. I took her every where I went. My sister would keep her while I worked at a Beauty Salon in Virginia part time. I also kept the tradition to cook my very first Christmas dinner and invite some family to eat over my house. I love looking at a Christmas tree while letting my thoughts flow in my mind. The holidays passed by that year and I continued going to work and school. Life was great I had even started dating again. Nothing serious but just clean fun. One of my Aunts had help me get a car because my Mom old car had broke down and got towed away. By the spring of 2003 I had found my own apartment in Sterling Virginia that was a two bedroom. It was a blessing to have housing assistance. Harmony's father had found out where I lived and got visitation to see Harmony. I eventually graduated from cosmetology school and began working as a cashier at Target until I received my cosmetology license. One day while shopping at the Salvation Army in Virginia I met a man from Ghana Accra. He offered to take me out to dinner. He was very dark complexion, tall, and had jet black wavy hair. He was really nice to me. We dated for a while and often went out to eat and parties a lot. I met his friends and family and he met Harmony, which he seemed to love. My nephew Chris moved in with me so he would keep an eye on Harmony while we went out together. He introduced me to his food and customs which I found exciting. Eventually we were together everyday. He would come over have dinner drink and relax plus talk He spoke the tree language in Africa so I was always glad to have someone so friendly and polite. We waited some time before we had sex, and that really help me find comfort in getting to know him. Eventually I had taken the State Board For Cosmetologist exam and passed the first time I had taken the test. So I left Target and began my career as a cosmetologist. I was so happy that my life was finally going in the direction I had envisioned. Harmony's father got jealous because I was in a knew relationship and stopped visiting with her. Chris moved out after about eight months and lived with Fonzo who was out of jail. Fonzo had got his Barbers license back and worked in the shop. My family had met my love interest and warned him to take care of me. I felt like a Queen. I had every thing that could make my heart happy and I made a decent living as a cosmetologist. I found out that I was pregnant again with my second child. I was scared because Mom was not living anymore. Harmony was three years old and I decided to name my daughter Gwen after my Mother. I would talk to my Mom alone and cry when I needed some one to talk too. My now fiancé proposed to me February of 2005 and asked me to marry him. I said yes, but I was still afraid but yet I was in love. Happiness was a big part of my life by this time. Someone was there and I felt that I could trust him. He was very easy to talk to and he always said thank God you are my very best friend. Life was going well even in spite me being pregnant. I seemed to just flow with every thing just fine. Harmony got her self into any and everything possible. She would take make up from my purse and put it on children at her daycare. She would break up any cigarettes she found at home, and she would talk to strangers. Harmony was a job in her self. After being pregnant for six months I stayed home for the remainder of the pregnancy. My craving was Mc Donalds fish sandwiches and fresh fruit. Gwen was ready to come out at thirty seven weeks. She was so cute and small when I held her. We moved to Ashburn VA by then into a three bedroom apartment and I was happy. The bills seemed to some how sky rocket and everything seemed so expensive. Money was very tight but I wanted to be ok and get married. I was excited but he seemed to be unhappy about getting married for some reason. He would seemingly start an argument each time I mentioned wedding planning. He started to work two jobs and I had to drop him off and pick him up because he did not drive and he did not have a drivers license. He started to become bitter and angry all the time. He would complain about anything and start arguments. Nothing seemed to make him happy but alcohol and money. I soon found out that he would cash his checks through his friend account because he did not a I.D. to work in the U.S. He said he could not sign Gwen birth certificate because he did not have a social security number. I was devastated and I did not trust him at all. I called one of my Aunts one night and explained everything to her about what was going on and it hurt like hell. I had never been through or seen any thing like this in my life. I also informed my father of what was happening. When he ran out of money he had spent my savings. I began to feel trapped and angry. When Gwen turned four months I woke up one morning and all of his clothes were gone and so was he. I did not know what to do or say. He actually broke my heart. I had two children, a deceased mother, and all of my family stayed in Maryland. It was hard for me cope because I was broke. Literally my electricity had got turned off and I had no choice but to leave the apartment and go and stay with Dad for a few weeks.

Chapter 5
Dad!

I could not find a job I was lost, ashamed, and overwhelmed. Dad was drunk a lot but everything he said to me made sense. He seemed as if he was hurt to know that someone whom he trusted had deceived me. A few weeks later I was contacted by him and he told me he had moved to Tennessee. I was startled but yet I was happy because I was still in love with him. He told me that he wanted me to come there and start over with him, I agreed. It seemed as if nothing was going right for me any way so I made preparations to go there with my children. I took the Greyhound bus from Washington D.C. and it took thirteen hours to get to Nashville Tennessee. I was afraid, excited, and scared. I had never traveled that far before and I wanted to have a new found sense of love again. The night we arrived my fiancé and his cousin picked us up. He had got a raggedy dodge neon from a friend for us to drive. We had to stay in a motel until we found an apartment. Two weeks later I began working the morning shift at BP Mapco and he worked evenings at a local warehouse in Antioch Tennessee. We soon found an apartment but we had no furniture. We rented furniture from rent a center but we did not have any beds. I was just happy that we had a place to live. Gwen began crawling by the time she was six months. Harmony was happy just to be in a new place. We argued but always seemed to make up. He had friends and family there so we could visit them at times. Deep inside I was nervous but I just wanted happiness and for everything to come together. I began to hate my job because my boss and I did not get along. She was very rude towards me and I felt hurt and afraid to say anything because I needed a place to work. Life went along I enrolled Harmony in school and I found another job at a salon. I soon found out that I pregnant again then I became upset. I had went to the doctor thinking I had the flu and I was six weeks pregnant. Gwen had just started walking. Everything seemed to go hay wire. The women at the salon was very jealous and began talking about me in front of my face. I could not find a daycare every one was filled, also I began to lose patience and went to apply for help at social services. That did help and I had to be at home with my children. They were happy but I felt miserable. I cut my hair and died it blonde but I still did not feel sexy. Life just seemed crazy, I began to crave coffee a lot during my pregnancy. It seemed as if everyone around me got pregnant as well so I was not alone. I did not feel sexy and I did not enjoy sex. I started to go to a class to start my own business, Provided by social services. This kept me busy at least. I was not happy about being pregnant until I found out that I was having a boy. On the sonogram his legs were wide open, I guess that was his way of telling Mom I am here. I always wanted a little boy for some reason. I planned to name him Frederick after his father. Things went well for a while and Harmony turned five and started school. She was a card, I had to go to school every week for a problem Harmony would cause for her class. I even had gotten into an argument with her teacher and principle for her stealing lolli pops from her teachers desk. Her teacher complained and Harmony was adjusting in her own way. She got spankings or time out but continued to act up in school. I was exhausted and very frustrated. I also began to ask questions about getting married and my fiancé carried worse than the children. So I said forget it. I just stop caring seeing that for some reason he did not care about us getting married. We had got a 1995 Nissan Maxima and I was more in love with the car than him by that time. So I found solace in driving and talking to God when I was alone. I had to pray a lot in order to get through each day. By this time my fiancé would talk to me anyway he felt like. He would threaten to slap the shit out of me if I did not shut up and be quiet. Again he became angry all the damn time. I still cursed him while he called me fat ass. I went through labor for one week before giving birth to Frederick on Christmas Day. I had contractions for a week, I remember cooking a big dinner on Christmas Eve and waking up in Labor Christmas Day. He was so beautiful and peaceful. Frederick didn't cry much just grunt. He looked like a little egg in his car seat and I was so happy when he was born. My fiancé would not hold him for two days because he was afraid about his circumcision.

Frederick one day started crying and I could not calm him down and I remember trying every thing possible to keep him from crying. I yelled at his father and cursed him telling him to help me with him. He held him and immediately Frederick stop crying, exhausted I could do nothing lie down. From that day forward he was happy to have a son. He walked around the house holding the baby naked and saying look at these balls. I would say put him down and laugh. I guess having more testosterone in the house got to his head. But then soon our happiness was once again stricken with anger and bitterness on his part. One day during a argument He punched me closed fist and began slapping me. Frederick was only a few weeks old. Then he would invite his friends over and after they left start this line of abuse. This started happening too often by now, and I grew tired and afraid and so did my children. It seemed as if I could not keep it together. I would at times have a stiff drink but even that did not help. I had got into a minor car accident a few weeks prior to Frederick being born and received a check from the insurance company. We bought a new bed and my fiancé just got more fueled more drunk and more abusive. One day while he went to work I went into his closet only to find his suit cases filled with his clothes. When he called home on his lunch break we started to curse each other. He got paranoid and came right home. He screamed and yelled and kicked open the room door, and began to hit me. We started fighting and I grabbed him tore his shirt completely down the middle and swung him against the wall. He got so fueled that he punched a hole in the wall of our bedroom. I could not take much more of this anymore. So not knowing what to and being tired and unable to rest a t night I told him to just leave. He packed up and walked out. I was afraid because again I had no income and Harmony began to tell me that she was afraid of him. So me being afraid for our lives I called my family and explained what had been happening. I then called the police filed a report and I had to be admitted into psychiatric treatment and social services had to keep my children because I had no family in Tennessee to come and pick up my children. I was devastated and I wanted to kill him. I could not believe how in God's name could I have sacrificed my love to a man so selfish and cruel. I went in the hospital hurt and angry, but I remember that I laughed a lot being around the other patients. That help me cope. I started to hallucinate at times and I would think that he was after me for some reason and I would cry. My

Aunt had told me that her and my cousin would come and pick my children up and me as well. She told me this for at least two weeks before she finally showed up. I was sent to a women's shelter eventually and I waited there for my family to show. Everyone was angry with my ex fiancé because He was less of a man in my folks eyes. Social workers seemed to not care about my needs at all. Nothing I said seemed to matter to them. They insisted that my Aunt keep my children. I was destroyed inside my heart. My children meant the world to me and I had no idea I would have to suffer in order to get custody of them again. My Aunt said that I could live with her when we appeared before the judge in court. She also said that she could help me with the children until I had got back on my feet. So I agreed to let her have temporary custody of my children. When coming back to D.C. I was so happy to be with my family again. When I arrived in my Aunt's home she began to act totally different to me. She looked at me and said "I am going to keep the children go out and take care of yourself". I looked at her and said that I thought I was going to live here with you and my children? I looked at her and she said I guess you can live with your father Amon. I was so hurt I could not say anything all I did was go to the car I drove which was the Maxima and drove away. She had used me to get custody of my children. I felt horrible and I became very angry with any and everyone. I moved in with Dad and I slept on the sofa. The court ordered supervised visitation and my Aunt and her children followed the order the way they felt like it. Some times I knocked at her door and she would not open it up for me. I became very furious and called the police on her. The police ordered for me to continue to follow the court order as opposed. I had found a job at a hair salon in Forestville and began to go to work. I also began to drink excessively when I was off from work. The more I got denied custody of my children the more I would get angry and drink. I still went to visitation but I started arguments with my cousins and my Aunt said that I could not come to her house anymore. So my cousin would bring my children to the park. Sometimes we ate at McDonalds but I could not take them home. Who knew my life would come to this because I sure didn't. After a while I began to smoke weed at my father house a lot. So I started to spiral down emotionally by this time. I took ecstacy pills and I began to snort cocaine. My life was in shambles because I began to hate who I had become. My relationship was over, I lost my children and I had to sleep on the sofa Oh I was a bitch to any one who got in my way. No one could feel this cold pain that I felt and my Aunt just intensified my feud. One day Fonzo and I got drunk and beat the hell out of each other. But this brought my brothers and sisters closer together. Everyone became so surprised at my Aunt and her actions. She began to get a check for each one of my children and I just did not know what to do. Several months later I lost complete control of everything including my job. I went back into the hospital very delusional and scared. My Dad was so upset when he found out I had done such strong drugs. He knew about the weed and alcohol but nothing else until I told him everything he was upset but I felt relieved that this was said and done. I was to be admitted into the hospital. This did not make me happy but my family was happy. Thinking that everything was ok in my life I was lying to myself. I was suicidal and I felt as if I did not want to live anymore. Needing help was not easy for me I had to crawl before I could walk. No one knew how I felt inside but God himself. I did not even understand what was wrong in my head. I felt sad a lot very angry and very lonely at this point in my life. I had to tell the doctors and nurses what was going on because I knew that my life had come to a holt. Losing energy and feeling guilty was not fun at all. I needed a plan. That is what I got help with a plan to conquer what was wrong. I was sent to a ten day detox center and from there to a rehab center in Laurel M.D. Leaving my Dad's house was a new experience and scary as well. I was afraid yet relieved I wanted my own home again, and I wanted my children back. The feeling of shame had crossed my mind because I could not believe that this was happening to me. Why did I lose so much and my cousin's that were my same age were moving on in their lives pretty well. This thought pondered in my mind always. I had to get a sponsor to help me along my path. Talking to other women in the program help me to accept what was going on and who really needed to change which was me. I cried, got angry, then ignore any one I felt I did not like. Being Maddy had become difficult and I did not understand a lot at the time.

But I learned quickly that the road that I had chose was not a good one. I was giving in to a life that truly did not want me. Using drugs brought out a mind in me that just did not care what any one thought or said or believed. I started to believe in others including myself. Feeling that it was ok to cry and talk about me helped my heart as well as my mind. I became in touch with my spirituality and that felt good. I was in a place that I should have been. I found a job and I was happy. I had to catch the bus around town after selling my Maxima for money, but I did not mind. Still having supervised visitation with my children made me upset so I filed for custody again with the D.C. superior court system. I had to work and that was real. I thought the court would just give me my children right back but to my surprise this wasn't so. I started to miss my Mom. I knew that if she had still been here the majority of these incidents would have never happened. My life is as it is. Many causes not to complain. Who I write about is who I really am and for some reason I'm no longer ashamed of my life. Moving in a house with five other strange women was not easy. This was where I had to live after living in a half way house for six months. The court system still did not increase my visitation at this time. I was off from drugs, alcohol, and I rented a room. I watched as other women's family brought their children over to spend weekends or visits with them and I could only go to McDonald's and eat with my children for thirty minutes. My sponsor went to court with me to support me and this had not even help. So I continued to work and go to meetings. After about eight months of this I grew tired. Women in the house started to turn against me and I began to become annoyed with the constant bickering and back stabbing that occurred in the home. Women that were miserable had started to fight against the positive people in our house. My Father had to have surgery and had not drank alcohol in two months prior to his surgery. I had to keep his car and help pay his bills for him while he was in the hospital. I started to feel sad and I began to get tired a lot. My job was not easy to keep by this time so I started looking for a new one. Dad condition had started to worsen and I became more stressed out. I could not live in a women's house and continue to help Dad. So I packed my things and I proceeded to move back home with Dad. I had been in search of a new beginning and I wanted my Father to live. I had lost one parent and I had not been in any position to lose another one. So I went on and did everything he needed done because I wanted my own life to get normal finally. I did keep my counselors that I had gained through the program and use their guidance and assistance. Life just seemed ok I guess but I did not know what to think by now. Everything seemed so off and it seemed as if I could not believe what was going on. Dad was getting ill and I felt worse.

He had supported me through out the program and all and now that no longer brought me happiness. Being home again brought on worries of getting my children back, and being able to properly raise them. I had started to miss them a great deal and I again went to the courthouse and applied for custody. As time went on I felt at ease. Dad could only move his right arm while he had no feeling in the left. Dad was often very quiet and peaceful. I had gained his trust again by staying on the right path and staying out of the streets. My brothers and sister supported me as well through out my new journey. The journey of independence. At this time I felt that God has done these things for a reason, to make me stronger, wiser, and a better person. I know that throughout this process no one knew or could know how I felt unless I told them, or they witnessed the same thing. My life is good and I began to see this and appreciate this. No one has blessed me the way God has. My father did get better after I lived with him throughout the year which is 2009 up until now. I have not had arguments with him and I have no longer been angry. Now I say that it is my time and thank God I am here today to tell my story to others who may have had struggles such as mine or even worse. You know I struggled to write this book because I needed confidence. How I got this confidence was through faith it seemed as if my life had ended at certain periods through out the years but I know now that this was a new start or new beginning. Now I believe that I am worth more than what the world think about me.

The New Me!

The new me has learned a lot through out my path, many days and nights I worried about if I could go through with this project. Oh many days I wanted to give up and many days I wanted to go on my patio and scream WHY ME! I only could handle but so much. I cried a lot while writing this book. This was not easy at all, I prayed then typed, I cried, then typed, I called my best friend then typed I wanted to get to the bottom of why my damn career has been hay wire. Certain jobs was no longer good enough and I lost a lot of jobs through out this process of writing this book. Actually nothing went the way I wanted it except for this book. I guess this was meant to be. Now I realize that this is what I was meant to have. A new life and new miracles in progress, my children are with me now in more ways than one. I am a achiever and I won't take this back neither should you. I am still single, sexy, and happy thank you Jesus. I know it may sound arrogant to some but we are who we work to become and no one knows us like we do so do me a favor please. Look in the mirror and shout I AM HERE!

Beauty

Beauty is your smile wear it

Beauty is your walk be it

Beauty is your talk say it

Beauty is your mind use it

Beauty is your name spell it

Beauty is your skin glow with it

Beauty is your buddy befriend it

Beauty is within you and me

Thanks Madalyn 2010

www.ingramcontent.com/pod-product-compliance
Lightning Source LLC
Chambersburg PA
CBHW051247120626
46547CB00014B/1832